SMART Board™ Lessons: Persuasive Writing

40 Ready-to-Use, Motivating Lessons on CD to Help You Teach
Essential Writing Skills

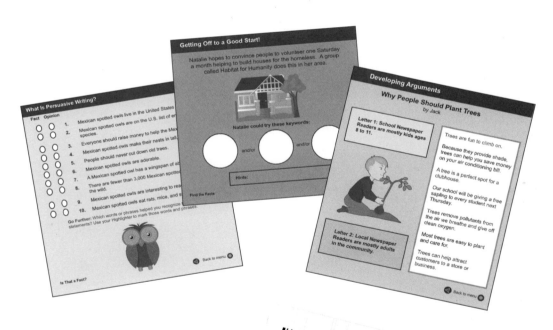

By Karen Kellaher

SMART™

SMART Notebook
content

Premium

New York • Toronto • London • Auckland • Sydney
Mexico City • New Delhi • Hong Kong • Buenos Aires

Teaching *Resources*

For Mom, one of the world's great persuasive artists

Text © 2011 by Karen M. Kellaher

Edited by Maria L. Chang and Betsy Henry Pringle

Illustrations by Kelly J. Brownlee

Cover design by Brian LaRossa

Book design by Rosanna Brockley

Art direction by Sarah Baynes

Design assistance by Catherine Chien, Aileen Morrow

Production by Jennifer Marx

SMART Board™ Lessons: Persuasive Writing
is produced by **becker&mayer!**, Bellevue, WA 98004

ISBN-13:-978-0-545-28512-4

ISBN-10: 0-545-28512-7

10832

All rights reserved.

Printed, manufactured, and assembled in Hong Kong, China

1 2 3 4 5 6 7 8 9 10   16 15 14 13 12 11

Contents

Introduction

Looking for a way to energize your writing curriculum? The perfect tool is hanging on your classroom wall! By using your SMART Board™ to teach writing genres and skills, you can bring the writing process to life and model how to form ideas, choose words, organize information, and much more. You will discover many advantages over more traditional methods:

- The SMART Board offers instant lesson engagement. Whether you are teaching about nouns, narratives, or Roman numerals, you will have students' immediate attention. Many of today's kids were computer literate even before they started school. They are accustomed to games and gadgets that respond to the touch of a fingertip. A SMART Board grabs their attention in a way that blackboards and handouts fail to do.

- Because it offers a large, interactive display and opportunities for collaborative learning, the SMART Board is a smart way to teach students 21st-century skills like working in teams, marking text electronically, synthesizing information, organizing data, interpreting visual aids, and evaluating Web sites. These skills are an increasingly important part of the standards in many states.

- The SMART Board is easy to use, even for technophobes. Using the board itself and the accompanying Notebook software is fairly intuitive. On the interactive whiteboard, you can do anything you can do on your computer screen—and then some. So even if you are just starting out, you can pull off a fun, effective lesson. The lessons on the attached CD will make it easy.

About the CD and Book

Make the most of SMART technology within your language arts curriculum. The SMART Notebook pages on the CD are a perfect way to teach writing skills because they allow you to model concepts and skills for the whole class. You can read and analyze examples of persuasive writing together, deciding what kinds of leads grab a reader's attention and what types of arguments are most convincing. You can move, highlight, underline, and change text right on the whiteboard. And best of all, you can save everything for later use or review. Distribute copies of the completed Notebook pages for students to have on hand as rule reminders.

The CD contains five units on persuasive writing. Each unit is on the CD as a Notebook file with several interactive pages. These pages take advantage of the bells and whistles SMART technology has to offer without being overwhelming to the SMART Board novice. You'll find opportunities to use the Creative Pens, on-screen keyboard, graphic organizers, cloning tools, drag-and-drop feature, and much more. Instructions for using each SMART tool are embedded in the lesson plans.

Each unit on the CD introduces writing skills in a gradual-release format. The first lesson in each unit introduces the topic, engages students' attention, and establishes what they already know. In the next few lessons, students collaboratively explore concrete skills related to the topic. In the last "lesson," students synthesize and apply what they have learned in a brief, independent assignment. You may choose to have students complete this final Your Turn! activity in class or as a homework assignment.

This book contains easy-to-use lessons corresponding to each CD unit. Lessons include objectives, pacing suggestions, and step-by-step directions for teaching with each SMART Notebook file on the CD. They also correlate with important language arts standards.

Tech Tips

Although the SMART Persuasive Writing CD was created using Notebook 10 software, you will be able to use the activities with older versions of the software. If you are still getting the hang of your SMART Board, be sure to look for the technology tips offered at various points throughout the units. However, the following is an overview of the main Notebook features you will be using.

 SMART Pens These are the black, red, green, and blue pens that came with your SMART Board. Use them to write directly on the screen in digital ink.

 Creative Pens A student favorite, this tool allows you to draw fun lines made of smiley faces, stars, rainbow stripes, and more.

 Magic Pen When students circle text or art with the Magic Pen, a spotlight focuses on the circled portion of the page. Everything else on the page goes dark temporarily. It's a dramatic way to focus attention on one element on a page!

 Eraser Like its old-fashioned counterpart, this eraser removes unwanted writing. It will work on text and lines created with the SMART pens. It will not work on typed text or art objects.

 On-Screen Keyboard If your students are adding text to a small field or simply prefer typing to writing freehand, use the on-screen keyboard. You can access it by touching the keyboard icon on the front tray of your SMART Board.

 Properties Tool In several of the activities in this book, you will be guided to use this feature to change the color or style of a SMART pen or to add color to a box.

 Screen Shade A teacher favorite, this tool allows you to cover part of a page while focusing attention on another part. Activate the shade by clicking on the Screen Shade icon on your toolbar. Deactivate it by clicking again. To gradually open a shade that covers your screen, use one of the circular buttons on the shade itself to drag the shade open.

What Is Persuasive Writing?

Use these engaging Notebook pages to introduce the purpose and characteristics of persuasive writing and to explore the many forms persuasive writing can take.

OBJECTIVES

Students will be able to:

✓ Analyze examples of persuasive writing.

✓ Understand the purpose and common elements of persuasive writing.

✓ Understand the importance of knowing one's audience.

TIME

About 3–4 class periods for Unit 1 (allow 15–20 minutes per lesson)

MEETING THE STANDARDS

This lesson correlates to the following writing standards for grades 3 through 6:

• Understand how writing can be adapted for different audiences and purposes.

• Recognize the elements common to persuasive text, including a thesis statement and arguments.

GETTING READY

Before students arrive, have your SMART Board ready to go. Load the SMART Persuasive Writing CD onto your host computer and copy the **1 What Is Persuasive Writing?** Notebook file onto your hard drive. Open the local file. The first interactive page, the *What Is Persuasive Writing?* menu, will appear on your SMART Board. To display the Notebook pages for each of the eight lessons in this unit, click on the button next to the name of the lesson.

INTRODUCING THE CONCEPT

Persuade Me

1. Display *Persuade Me* on the SMART Board. To begin, ask students to think about what we mean by the word *persuade*. Elicit definitions from the class. Ask students to think about times they have tried to persuade family members or friends to do something (for example, maybe they recently lobbied to see a new movie or get a new video game). Point out that in persuasive writing, the writer's purpose is not to inform or entertain, but to persuade readers. The writer tries to get the reader to think or act in a certain way.

2. Read the directions on the page together. Then click on the right arrow button to go to the next page. Have a student read aloud the first piece of text. Together, discuss what the letter writer wants the reader of the letter to think or do. If you wish, have students use the SMART highlighter pen to highlight the parts of the letter that help them identify the writer's mission. Invite the student to use a SMART pen to write this mission on the lines below the question.

3. Invite a second volunteer to click on the red box below the lines. The writer's persuasive mission will be revealed. Discuss whether students were on target in identifying the writer's purpose.

4. Repeat steps 2 and 3 with the pieces of text on the next two pages.

5. Guide students to notice that the writer's mission statement is clearer in some examples than in others. For example, in the letter to the robot maker, the writer clearly states, "I am sure you will agree to replace my robot or give me a full refund." But in the sign in the grocery store, the writer gently hints at what he or she wants shoppers to do (use canvas bags). Discuss how a clear persuasive statement helps make writing more persuasive.

6. If you wish, save your class's work and make a copy of the pages for each student to keep in his or her writing folder.

 TECH TIP

If students have trouble writing with the SMART pen, check that they are holding the stylus correctly. If a student's wrist or hand rubs against the board while writing, the writing may appear garbled and illegible. When using a SMART pen, only the stylus tip should make contact with the SMART Board.

A Reason to Write

1. Ask students to recall examples of persuasive writing they have seen. Discuss their examples, pointing out that persuasive text can take many forms (letters, editorials, advertisements, speeches, etc.) and topics. Explain that students can check if a piece of text is meant to be persuasive by asking themselves, *Does the writer want the reader to do something?*

2. Display *A Reason to Write* on the SMART Board and read the directions together. Click on the right arrow button to go to the next page. Have a student read the first example and decide if Sarah's writing will involve persuasion. Discuss clues in the example that helped the student come to that conclusion. Then have the student click on the picture (the birthday cake, in this example) to see if he or she was right. If the writing task is persuasive, the picture will spin. If the writing task is not persuasive, the picture will remain still.

3. Repeat step 2 with the other examples on this page and the next. You will find that the following are examples of persuasive writing:

   - Sarah's birthday party speech

   - The soccer league's advertisement

   - Oliver's movie blog

   - The bakery employees' letter to their boss

4. For the writing tasks that students decide are not persuasive in nature, discuss what the purpose of the writing is (for example, to inform or entertain).

5. Invite students to brainstorm other examples of persuasive writing—either real or imagined—and share their ideas with the class.

Audience Matters

1. To engage students, present them with these two scenarios:

   - Imagine that you want to start earning an allowance in exchange for doing chores around the house. To whom would you talk? *(Most likely responses are parent or guardian)*

   - Imagine that you wanted the school library to purchase a popular new book series. To whom would you go? *(Responses may include the school librarian, principal, or board of education)*

   Point out that students would approach different groups of people for these very different purposes. Explain that identifying one's audience is an important step in persuasive writing.

2. Display *Audience Matters* on the SMART Board and read the introduction and example as a class.

3. Click on the right arrow to display the first piece of text. Drag the red Pull arrow from the side to read the directions. Divide students into small groups and have each group read the writing task on the screen. Have each group decide whom the most appropriate audience would be for the task.

4. When groups are finished, invite a group to share its thinking about audience for the task. Have a representative from the group approach the SMART Board and drag the magnifying glass over the four options. Only the appropriate audience will be visible through the glass.

5. Repeat steps 3 and 4 with the remaining writing tasks.

6. Discuss how identifying the audience can help a writer be more persuasive. *(He or she can choose arguments, words, and a tone that will appeal to that audience. For example, we might encourage a friend to see a "rockin'" new movie, but we would probably stick to standard English in a letter to the local newspaper.)*

 TECH TIP

If students have trouble dragging and dropping the magnifying glass image, demonstrate the process yourself. Explain that students should not take their finger off the SMART Board once they have touched the image they wish to move. The drag function works best when the user's finger stays in contact with the board.

The Power of Persuasion (Part 1)

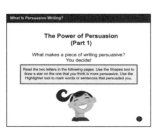

1. In this activity, students will decide for themselves what makes a piece of writing persuasive. Display *The Power of Persuasion (Part 1)* on the SMART Board and read the directions aloud. Click on the right arrow and invite a student volunteer to read aloud the first letter to Principal Tanner. Together, identify what the writer wants Principal Tanner to think or do. *(Stop entertaining the idea of school uniforms)* Discuss whether he or she makes a good case and why.

2. Click on the right arrow again and have another volunteer read aloud the second letter to Principal Tanner. Guide students to notice that this letter writer has the same goal as the first letter writer. Together, compare and contrast the two letters. Ask students to decide which letter is more persuasive and why. Some things students might notice include:

   Letter 1

   - Has spelling errors.
   - Is disorganized.
   - Uses words like *horrible*, which might be insulting to the principal.
   - Does not offer any facts to back up the opinion.
   - Goes off topic.

   Letter 2

   - Is free of spelling and grammar errors.
   - Is organized into paragraphs with main ideas.
   - Has a catchy beginning.
   - States an opinion clearly and politely.
   - Backs up the opinion with solid reasons and facts.
   - Repeats the opinion at the end of the letter.
   - Sticks to the topic.

3. Display both letters on the SMART Board at the same time, using the Dual/Single Page Display tool ▭. To do so, go to the toolbar on your SMART Board display and click on the icon that resembles a computer monitor with two pages on it. Now, the two pages should appear on your board side by side.

4. Following your discussion, have a student use the Shapes tool to place a star on the more persuasive letter *(Letter 2)*. Take a moment to demonstrate the Shapes feature of Notebook. Simply touch the Shapes tool with a finger and select the star shape. Then touch where you want to put the star and drag your finger to create the shape. You can use the Properties tool to color the star.

5. Invite the students to use the SMART highlighter to highlight parts of the letter that were particularly persuasive to them. (You may want to switch back to Single Page Display to focus on just the letter.)

The Power of Persuasion (Part 2)

1. In this activity, students will use the qualities they noticed in the persuasive letter in Part 1 to complete a graphic organizer. As you discuss the directions and study the graphic organizer together, you may wish to use the Dual/Single Page Display tool to display both Letter 2 and the graphic organizer simultaneously.

2. Display *The Power of Persuasion (Part 2)* on the SMART Board and review students' reasons for choosing the second letter in Part 1. Guide students to make generalizations about good persuasive writing based on those reasons.

3. Have students use the SMART pens to write a generalization in each box of the graphic organizer. (You will probably need to switch back to Single Page Display to make it easier for students to write in the boxes. To do so, simply touch on the Dual/Single Page Display tool again.) Some possible observations include:

> - Starts by grabbing the reader's attention.
> - Clearly states the writer's opinion (what he or she wants the reader to do or think).
> - Gives reasons and facts to support the opinion.
> - Repeats the writer's opinion at the end.
> - Is organized into paragraphs with main ideas.
> - Sticks to the topic.

4. If students make more than six observations, they can easily add boxes to the graphic organizer. Simply click on the Shapes tool and select the rectangle shape. Click and drag to draw a large rectangle. To connect the rectangle to the organizer, click on the Line tool and select a simple straight line. Click and drag to draw a line between the new rectangle and the center circle of the organizer.

5. Save your class's work and make copies for students' writing folders.

 TECH TIP

If you need to resize a box once you have placed it on the page, never fear! Simply touch the selector tool (the plain black arrow) and use this tool to select the box you have drawn. Touch the white resizing circle on the bottom right of the box and pull down and to the right.

Is That a Fact?

1. Display *Is That a Fact?* on the SMART Board and read the introduction and examples on the page. Explain to students that both facts and opinions are vital in persuasive writing. We write to express an opinion—and convince others to share that opinion—but we must back up that opinion with facts in order to win others over.

2. Click on the right arrow to go to the next page. Drag the Pull arrow on the upper right-hand corner of the page to read the directions. Demonstrate how to use the Creative Pen to put a smiley face on the page. With a finger, click on the Creative Pen icon and select the smiley face option. Then touch the SMART Board once to put a single smiley face on the page.

3. Have students read aloud the first statement and decide whether it is a fact or an opinion. If students are unsure, have them discuss whether (and how) the statement could be proven true. For instance, in the examples on the previous page, students read that "Daniella is 4 feet tall." This statement could be proved by measuring Daniella or looking at her medical chart. Therefore, it is a fact.

4. Call on a student to use the Creative Pen to put a smiley face in the appropriate bubble. Repeat until students have identified all of the statements as facts or opinions. *(Statements 1, 2, 4, 7, 8, and 10 are facts; 3, 5, 6, and 9 are opinions.)*

5. Point out the Go Further prompt at the bottom of the page. Explain that certain kinds of words signal to readers that a statement is an opinion. Abstract adjectives like *better* and *nice* are opinion signal words. So are words like *should*. Challenge students to revisit the opinion statements they found and use the Highlighter tool to mark any opinion signal words or phrases.

6. Save your class's work and make a copy for each student's writing folder.

TECH TIP

When using the Creative Pen to place a single smiley face (or other shape) on the screen, tap the SMART Board with the pen instead of pushing down. A quick tap places a single shape on the screen.

Persuasive Puzzle

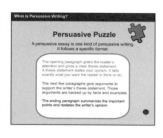

1. Display *Persuasive Puzzle* on the SMART Board. Point out that persuasive writing often takes the form of a five-paragraph essay. (Even many letters to newspaper editors follow this tried-and-true format.) In this format, each paragraph has a specific job, as outlined on the page. Read and discuss the description of a persuasive essay's opening paragraph, supporting paragraphs, and ending paragraph.

2. Click on the right arrow to go to the next page. Then drag the Pull arrow on the left side to read the directions together. Explain that students will piece together a five-paragraph persuasive essay about electronic textbooks. All five of the paragraphs are on the page, but they are out of order. Students will put the essay back in correct order, remembering each paragraph's job and then locating the paragraph that meets those requirements.

3. Review the description of a persuasive essay's opening paragraph. Then study the five paragraphs on the page and have students find the paragraph that would work best as an opening paragraph. Have a student volunteer drag the paragraph next to "Opening Paragraph."

4. Review the description of the supporting-argument paragraphs. Point out that persuasive essays often have three main supporting arguments, though there is no firm rule about the number of arguments. For some reason, readers tend to expect important things to come in threes. (Think of mystery clues and fairy tale wishes!)

5. Have students identify the three paragraphs that appear to be supporting arguments. Look for sequencing words (like *one reason*, *another reason*, and *finally*) to put the paragraphs in order. Have a volunteer drag them in order next to "Supporting Paragraphs."

6. Review the role of the ending paragraph, then drag this paragraph into place.

7. Save your class's work and make a copy for each student's writing folder.

What Is Persuasive Writing? Your Turn!

1. Print and make copies of *What Is Persuasive Writing? Your Turn!* Display both Notebook pages on the SMART Board and distribute copies of the worksheets. Explain that students will complete this page on their own to apply what they have learned about persuasive writing so far.

2. Review the directions with students, explaining that they will read a persuasive letter and:

> • Identify the writer and intended audience.
>
> • Identify what the writer wants readers to think or do.
>
> • Find the three arguments that the writer uses and details to support those arguments.
>
> • Evaluate the persuasiveness of the letter.

3. Have students complete the exercise in class or as a homework assignment. Invite volunteers to share their work with the class

Getting Off to a Good Start!

In this series of interactive Notebook pages, students learn to choose topics, do research, and take a stand. They also get pointers on tackling that all-important first paragraph!

OBJECTIVES

Students will be able to:

✓ Use real problems and issues they care about to form persuasive essay topics.

✓ Thoughtfully choose sides, given a persuasive essay prompt.

✓ Use key words to research their persuasive topics.

✓ Write a first paragraph that includes a strong thesis statement and attention-grabbing beginning.

TIME

About 3–4 class periods for Unit 2 (allow 15–20 minutes per lesson)

MEETING THE STANDARDS

This lesson correlates to the following writing standards for grades 3 through 6:

• Apply a variety of prewriting strategies in order to generate and structure ideas.

• Conduct research on issues by generating ideas and questions.

• Use a variety of technological and information resources.

• Create interesting leads.

• Write persuasive text that establishes a simple controlling idea (thesis).

GETTING READY

Before students arrive, have your SMART Board ready to go. Load the SMART Persuasive Writing CD onto your host computer and copy the **2 Getting Off to a Good Start** Notebook file onto your hard drive. Open the local file. The first interactive page, the *Getting off to a Good Start* menu, will appear on your SMART Board. To display the Notebook pages for each of the eight lessons in this unit, click on the button next to the name of the lesson.

Start Right

1. Display *Start Right* on the SMART Board. Tell students that before a writer begins drafting a persuasive essay or letter, there are certain steps he or she should take. Explain that for this activity, students get to be the "teachers" and evaluate whether imaginary students in the class have followed those steps and are ready to write.

2. Discuss the prerequisites for persuasive writing listed on the page:

> **Choose a topic that you care about.** Ask: *Why do you think it is important that you care about your topic? What if I just told all of you to write about why the price of potatoes should be lower?* Guide students to understand that when a writer cares about his or her topic, that passion is sure to shine through in the essay or letter.
>
> **Do research to learn the facts.** Ask: *Is this surprising to you? Why do you think persuasive essays need facts?* Point out that opinions need to be grounded in facts in order to carry any real weight.
>
> **Take a stand.** Ask: *Why is it important to think through exactly what you want your readers to think or do? If you sound wishy-washy, what will your readers think?*

3. Read the directions with the class. Then click on the right arrow to go to the next page. Invite a volunteer to read aloud Sarabel's proposal for her persuasive essay. Together, use the three prerequisites to evaluate whether Sarabel is ready to start the writing process. Ask students to consider whether Sarabel has a topic that she cares about *(she has a topic that she cares about, but it is fuzzy)*, has done research to learn the facts *(no)*, and has taken a stand *(no, she does not say what she wants readers to think or do)*. Because Sarabel has not met all three requirements, have the student volunteer put an *X* in the box by Sarabel's name.

4. Repeat step 3 with the remaining two topic proposals. Students will discover that Trish and Jason have clear topics that they care about, have done research (via books and Web searches), and have taken a stand. Student volunteers can put a checkmark by these students' names.

5. Click on the right arrow to display the teacher's notebook. Move the notebook aside to see if the teacher agrees.

Turn Problems Into Topics

1. Display *Turn Problems Into Topics* on the SMART Board. Guide students to understand that many persuasive essay topics spring from real problems that people experience or witness. Sometimes, the writer wants to make people aware of a new problem and recommend a solution. Other times, the writer addresses a problem that is well known and controversial. In those cases, there are usually many possible solutions and the writer argues why one particular solution is the best.

2. Click on the right arrow to go to the next page. Divide the class into small groups and have them use the chart to brainstorm problems that they have noticed. If they have trouble getting started, offer a few examples of your own:

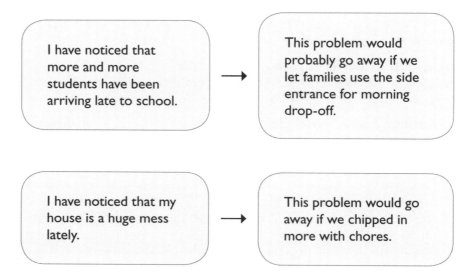

3. Invite someone from each group to discuss their ideas. Have students use the SMART pens to fill in the charts on both pages.

4. Discuss students' examples, modeling how the proposed solution to each problem could be transformed into an opinion statement telling what readers should think or do. For example, the late-arrival problem mentioned above could be used for an essay arguing that the school should open the side entrance in the morning. The messy house problem could turn into an essay arguing why kids should help with household chores.

5. Save your class's work and make a copy for each student's writing folder.

Make a Wish

1. Display *Make a Wish* on the SMART Board and read the introduction and directions together. Explain that this activity is another fun way to generate ideas for persuasive writing. Click on the right arrows over the next five pages so students can read all of the prompts in the thought balloons. Have students spend a few minutes responding to the prompts in their writing notebooks or on scrap paper.

2. When students have finished brainstorming, elicit a few sample responses for each prompt. Use the SMART pens to write one or two examples inside each thought balloon.

3. Discuss how a writer could turn each "wish" into a persuasive essay. For example, if a student said that the world would be a better place if people did more to help one another, he or she could argue that schools should require students to do community service.

4. If your students are planning their own persuasive essays at this time, pause after completing this lesson to have students reflect on some of the topics they have explored. Have each student share his or her chosen topic with the class. Make sure each student can phrase his or her topic as something he or she wants readers to think or do.

5. Help students hone topics that are too large, vague, or unrealistic. If a problem or wish is very large (such as reducing global warming or eliminating poverty), encourage students to choose one reasonable thing they will ask readers to do about it. Remind students that the more "doable" a message sounds, the more likely it is that readers will be convinced.

6. Save your class's work and make a copy of the pages for each student's writing folder.

 TECH TIP

Once in a while, consider having students type their responses onto the screen instead of using the SMART pens. Activate your on-screen keyboard by touching the keyboard key on your SMART Board tray or by choosing the keyboard icon in your toolbar.

Choosing Sides

1. Explain that sometimes students may be asked to write persuasively on a topic that is not of their own choosing. For example, prompts on standardized tests routinely give students a debate and ask them to take and defend a stand. In such "write on demand" situations, it is important to think through both sides of the issue before choosing a position.

2. Display *Choosing Sides* on the SMART Board and read the directions together. Discuss what a *ban* on homework means. Acknowledge that most students' initial reaction will be to support a ban on homework, but encourage the class to think through both sides before they decide. Then, explain that they will brainstorm arguments both in support of and in opposition to a ban on homework.

3. Click on the right arrow to go to the next page. Under "Yes," have student volunteers use the SMART pens to record arguments that would support such a ban. Sample arguments might include:

   - Kids are busy with sports and other activities.
   - Kids need down time with their families.
   - Too much homework means kids stay up later than they should.
   - Kids have plenty of time to learn during the school day.

4. Under "No," have students write arguments against a homework ban. Such arguments might include:

   - Homework helps kids review what they learned in school.
   - Homework keeps kids out of trouble.
   - Homework shows parents what kids are learning.

5. After you have completed both columns, click on the right arrow to take a class tally and see where students stand on the issue now. Invite students to approach the SMART Board one at a time and use the Creative Pen to stamp a smiley face icon next to "Yes" or "No." Students can access the Creative Pen by clicking on the Creative Pen icon with a finger and selecting the smiley face option. Note that only the first student will need to do this. The smiley face will stay activated until you click back on the selector (plain black arrow).

6. If any students changed their minds on this issue, discuss which arguments were most persuasive to them. Point out that even if students did not change their minds, brainstorming both sides of an issue can be useful in building a persuasive argument. Knowing the "other side" helps us address any concerns or questions our readers might have.

7. Save your class's work and make a copy of the pages for each student's writing folder.

Find the Facts

1. Pose this question to students: *Let's say I wanted our school to have more fire drills and offered you the following two arguments: (a) Fire drills are a good idea. (b) Studies show that school and office building fire drills helped save 12 lives last year. Which argument would you find more convincing?* Guide students to understand that facts are crucial to persuasive writing.

2. Ask students to think about their own topics and name some resources they might use to find information. Point out that the Internet is an excellent source of information, as long as you know how to conduct an efficient search. Explain that the words you enter into a search engine when you do a Web search are known as *keywords*.

3. Display *Find the Facts* on the SMART Board and read the directions. Click on the right arrow to read the first essay topic. Work with students to brainstorm some keywords that Jack could use to learn more about the dangers of cell-phone use while driving. Write students' ideas in the circles, then let students use the SMART eraser to reveal possible keywords inside the Hint box.

4. Repeat step 3 for Natalie's research on Habitat for Humanity and Julio's research on nutritious school lunches.

5. Discuss how using more than one keyword can help a writer narrow a search. For example, if Jack (in example 1) typed in *cell phone*, he'd find thousands of sites with many different purposes. He'd have to evaluate every single one to see if it related to the safety of cell-phone use while driving. But if Jack included the keywords *driving* and/or *safety* along with *cell phone* in his search, he would be directed to sites that focused on those areas.

6. If time permits, take a moment to do one of the searches described in this section. If your host computer is Internet ready, you can display your school-approved search engine right on your SMART Board. Compare the results you get using different combinations of keywords.

7. Review with students some of the ways they can tell if a Web site is a reliable source of facts for their persuasive essay. Point out that sites run by the government end in the suffix *.gov*, while sites run by nonprofit organizations end in *.org*, and school-connected sites end in *.edu*. These tend to be more trustworthy than sites hosted by individuals or companies.

8. Have students jot down some keywords they can use to search for information related to their own persuasive essay topics. Later, have them conduct their research and take notes.

9. Explain that being informed about one's topic is an important ingredient in the art of persuasion. It shows that the writer is an "expert." The ancient Greeks called this ingredient *ethos*. Let students know that they'll be learning about the other two ingredients in later lessons.

Smart Starts

1. Share with students that the beginning of an essay is often called the *lead*, or the *hook*. Explain that just as the baited hook on a fishing line lures fish in, the first lines of an essay should draw in readers and make them want to keep reading.

2. Display *Smart Starts* on the SMART Board and read the directions. Then click on the right arrow to read aloud Tom's essay topic. Explain that behind the colorful boxes on the next page are four interesting ways that Tom could begin his essay. Read the description of the first type of lead, Question, and invite students to think of a question that Tom might start with. After a few examples, have a student volunteer drag the orange box aside to reveal the hidden example.

3. Repeat step 2 with the remaining three types of leads: Wordplay, Just the Facts, and Imagine That. For each one, have students think of an example or two before revealing the example that Tom wrote.

4. Have students vote on which of Tom's leads they like best. Use the Magic Pen to circle the winning lead. (Watch students' faces as a spotlight shines on the winning lead and the rest of the page fades out of view!)

5. Finally, have students turn and talk briefly with a partner about some lead ideas for their own persuasive essays. Encourage them to try different kinds of openings before settling on a favorite.

 TECH TIP

Don't forget to put your tools away when you are through with them! After you use a tool like the Magic Pen, be sure to go back to the selector tool (plain black arrow) before continuing with other tasks.

Make a Statement!

1. Display *Make a Statement!* on the SMART Board and read the introduction. Guide students to understand that once they have grabbed readers' attention with a compelling lead, it is time to "reel in" those readers and get them to think or act in a particular way. For that reason, persuasive essays always give a clear opinion statement in the first paragraph. This is known as the *thesis statement.*

2. Click on the right arrow to read aloud the beginning of the first sample essay, "My Earth Day Challenge." Then read the three possible thesis statements. Have students discuss the pros and cons of each statement. Ask: *Which statement most clearly tells readers what they should think or do? Which statement sounds like a reasonable request?* Once students have chosen a thesis statement, have a volunteer drag the selected text into the essay box.

3. Point out that the third thesis statement, "Plant just one small tree and do our planet an enormous favor," works best because it is specific and clear and asks readers to do something reasonable. Readers might resist the idea of planting 100 trees, but planting one tree does not sound so difficult.

4. Repeat step 2 with the remaining two essays on the following pages, "Longer Recess, Please!" and "Allow This Site." Discuss why students chose the thesis statement they did for each essay. For "Longer Recess, Please!" the second thesis statement works best. The first option is too outrageous (a whole hour of lunch recess?) and unlikely to win over readers. The third option is unclear: What precisely does the writer want people to do? For "Allow This Site," the third statement choice is the most specific and reasonable.

5. Point out to students that in the "Longer Recess, Please!" example, the writer mentions his or her main arguments (kids will feel better, learn better) in the thesis statement. If we were able to read the next few paragraphs, one paragraph would very likely talk about ways kids would feel better, and one would talk about ways kids would learn better. Summarizing the main arguments in the thesis—even if it means including a second sentence—is a fantastic way to let readers know what to expect in the rest of the essay. While it is not absolutely essential, many elementary teachers find it instructive to require students to follow this practice. It helps develop the habit of organizing an essay into argument-themed paragraphs.

EXTENDED LEARNING

Getting Off to a Good Start: Your Turn!

1. Print and make copies of *Getting Off to a Good Start: Your Turn!* Display the Notebook pages on the SMART Board and distribute copies of the worksheets. Explain that students will complete these pages on their own, either in class or for homework, to apply what they have learned about starting a persuasive essay.

2. Review the directions with students, explaining that students will:

> • Choose a topic (if they have not done so already).
>
> • Brainstorm keywords for researching their topic.
>
> • Write a clear opinion or thesis statement.
>
> • Try different ways to begin their essay.

If you wish, instruct students to write a rough draft of their first paragraph.

3. Once students have completed their assignments, invite volunteers to share their work with the class.

Developing Arguments

In this series of Notebook pages, students dive into the body of a persuasive essay and learn how to build arguments supported by facts and examples.

OBJECTIVES

Students will be able to:

- ✓ Generate strong arguments for a persuasive topic.
- ✓ Support arguments with facts, examples, definitions, and statistics.
- ✓ Match arguments to an intended audience.
- ✓ Put arguments and details in their own words.

TIME

About 3–4 class periods for Unit 3 (allow 15–20 minutes per lesson)

MEETING THE STANDARDS

This lesson correlates with the following writing standard for grades 3 through 6:

- Understand how the intended audience affects the writing process.
- Present clear analyses of issues, supporting positions with well-developed arguments.
- Develop arguments with effective use of details and evidence.

GETTING READY

Before students arrive, have your SMART Board ready to go. Load the SMART Persuasive Writing CD onto your host computer and copy the **3 Developing Arguments** Notebook file onto your hard drive. Open the local file. The first interactive page, the *Developing Arguments* menu, will appear on your SMART Board. To display the Notebook pages for each of the eight lessons in this unit, click on the button next to the name of the lesson.

INTRODUCING THE CONCEPT

What Makes a Good Argument?

1. Display *What Makes a Good Argument?* on the SMART Board and read the introduction aloud. Explain that the body, or middle, of a persuasive essay or letter is made up of arguments or reasons why the writer's opinion makes sense. There are usually (but not always) at least three main arguments, and each one is supported by details. Remind students of the ancient Greek approach to persuasion. They have already learned that being well-informed provides *ethos*, or a good reputation. As they learn about arguments and supporting details, they will explore the ingredient of *logos*, or logic.

2. Read the directions in the box and then click on the right arrow to read the first essay topic. Challenge students to think of three arguments for the opinion statement listed on each of the following pages. Use the SMART pen to write each argument in a text box. Some ideas are listed below.

Why every classroom should have computers:

- Students will need strong computer skills for the future.
- Games and Web sites teach math, reading, and more.
- Teachers can use e-mail to communicate with families.

Why organized sports are good for kids:

- Kids learn teamwork and cooperation.
- Kids get exercise to help them stay fit.
- Sports give kids something to do after school and on weekends.

Why kids should have household chores:

- Kids share the house so they should share the responsibilities.
- Kids need to learn to pick up after themselves since they will live on their own one day.
- Families are busier than ever, and parents don't have time to do all the work.

3. For each topic, discuss the order in which the arguments should appear. It is a good idea to make sure stronger arguments appear first and last, with the weakest argument sandwiched in the middle.

4. If students are working on their own persuasive essays at this time, encourage them to try this activity with their own topic. If students cannot think of enough arguments, allow a minute or two for students to share their ideas in small groups. A fresh perspective is often all that is needed.

TECH TIP

If students' pen strokes are not showing up in the right spots, it may be a sign that your SMART Board needs to be reoriented. Orienting ensures that your board is properly aligned and that finger taps, pen strokes, and other tasks will show up exactly where you want them. It is especially important to reorient frequently if you use a portable SMART Board. To orient, look on the startup menu of your Notebook software. The process takes about ten seconds.

INTERACTIVE LEARNING

All in the Details

1. Display *All in the Details* on the SMART Board. Explain that this lesson explores some of the different kinds of details writers can use to support their arguments. Read the introduction and directions together, then click on the right arrow to read the first clue.

2. Have a student volunteer read the clue, pausing for the scrambled word. Encourage students to raise their hands when they think they have unscrambled the word. Select a volunteer to come up to the SMART Board and move the letters around to form the correct word.

3. Once you have unscrambled the first word (*DEFINITION*), have your student volunteer move the globe aside to see how Tia used that type of detail. Explain that definitions are useful when writing about complicated topics or topics that may be unfamiliar to most readers.

4. Repeat steps 2 and 3 for the three remaining scrambled clues on the following pages. The scrambled words are as follows:

> DEFINITION: Tells what a word or idea means
>
> FACT: Any statement that can be proved true
>
> STATISTIC: A piece of data that uses math, such as an average or percentage
>
> EXAMPLE: A specific, real-life instance of an idea

5. Have students share with the class some details that they plan on using to support the arguments in their own essays.

6. Point out that it is always a good idea to credit a source when sharing a statistic or unusual fact. Credit can be given with phrases such as, "According to researchers at . . ." or "One study at (name place) showed that . . ."

Perfect Paragraphs

1. Start your lesson by asking students why we use paragraphs when we write. Guide them to understand that paragraphs let writers (and readers) focus on a single important idea at a time. In persuasive writing, we use a new paragraph for each argument that we offer.

2. Display *Perfect Paragraphs* on the SMART Board and read the directions. Then click on the right arrow to go to the next page. Direct students' attention to the red paragraph symbol and demonstrate how the symbol *clones*, or copies, itself when you try to drag it from its spot on the page.

3. Read aloud the model essay, "Wear a Helmet!" After your initial reading, ask students if they can identify spots where Darren should have started a new paragraph. As a student identifies a spot, read aloud the first sentence of the new paragraph and ask the student to explain why a new paragraph should begin there. Guide students to see that a new paragraph should begin each time we introduce a new main idea.

4. Let your student volunteer drag the paragraph symbol to the appropriate spot on the page. Repeat until students have identified all three places where a new paragraph should begin, not including the first sentence. (*The paragraph symbol should come before the 3rd, 8th, and 12th sentences.*)

5. Have students revisit the newly identified paragraphs to recall Darren's three main arguments for wearing helmets. Invite volunteers to use the SMART pens to write these arguments on the following page.

6. If you wish, save your class's work and make a copy of the pages for each student's writing folder.

 **TECH TIP**

If your students enjoyed using the paragraph symbol that automatically copied itself, you might want to work this fun function into other lessons you do on the SMART Board. You can use the Infinite Cloner tool to let students make unlimited copies of almost anything—words, pictures, symbols, etc. Just select the item you wish to clone and go to the drop-down menu that appears in the top right corner of the item. Scroll down to Infinite Cloner.

Detail Matchup

1. Display *Detail Matchup* on the SMART Board. Explain that in the last lesson, students worked with paragraphs that were already written. In this activity, they will drag and drop details to form new paragraphs. Review the directions together and then click on the right arrow.

2. Read aloud the main ideas in the colored boxes on the next three pages. For each of the main ideas, have a student volunteer find a supporting detail in the column on the right and drag it to the main idea it best supports.

3. Repeat until all of the details have been placed beneath a main idea. Your boxes will look something like this:

> **One reason teachers should hold class outside once in a while is that sunlight is important for good health.**
>
> • Being exposed to a few minutes of natural sunlight every day gives the body vitamin D, which is important for strong bones.
>
> • Being outside during the day improves sleep, an important ingredient for good health.
>
> • Outdoor time helps the brain produce chemicals called *endorphins*, which are important for mental health.

> **A second reason to occasionally move classes outdoors is that it offers chances to learn about nature.**
>
> • During a science lesson, kids could notice different kinds of leaves.
>
> • They could search for examples of insects or observe the day's weather.
>
> • Even in a city, the great outdoors has something to teach us!

> **Finally, going outside for 30 minutes or so can give kids a much-needed boost of energy.**
>
> • When they sit at a desk for hours at a time, it is common for kids to grow bored.
>
> • A change in scenery helps kids focus again.

4. If you wish, save your class's work and make a copy of the pages for each student's writing folder.

Reach Your Audience

1. Ask students to imagine that they need to borrow a quarter to get a snack from a candy machine. What would they say if they were asking a younger brother or sister? (*I promise to share; etc.*) What would they say if they were asking a parent? (*I promise not to eat it before dinner; etc.*) Point out that we sometimes choose different arguments for different audiences.

2. Display *Reach Your Audience* on the SMART Board and read the directions on the page together. Emphasize that the writer has the same topic and thesis statement for each newspaper letter that he is writing. However, his arguments may vary since he has two distinct audiences. Have students identify the two audiences.

3. Click on the right arrow to go to the next page. Invite a student volunteer to touch the line/arrow tool on the Toolbar and select a line. (Students will probably be drawn to the brightly colored dashed lines on the menu.)

4. Read aloud the first argument in the list and decide as a class which audience it would be best for. Have your volunteer draw a line from the audience to the argument by touching and dragging with a finger.

5. Repeat step 4 for the remaining six arguments in the list. Use a different color or line style for arguments directed at the second audience. The results will vary from class to class. As long as students can explain why they think a particular argument would matter to an audience, you're on the right track! A general idea of how the arguments may break down appears below.

> ### Arguments for the school newspaper (for kids):
>
> - Trees are fun to climb on.
> - A tree is a perfect spot for a clubhouse.
> - Our school will be giving a free sapling to every student next Thursday.
> - Trees remove pollutants from the air we breathe and give off clean oxygen.
> - Most trees are easy to plant and care for.

> ### Arguments for the local newspaper (for adults):
>
> - Because they provide shade, trees can help you save money on your air-conditioning bill.
> - Trees remove pollutants from the air we breathe and give off clean oxygen.
> - Most trees are easy to plant and care for.
> - Trees can help attract customers to a store or business.

6. Save your class's work and make a copy for each student's writing folder.

TECH TIP

If you are looking for a particular tool (such as the line/arrow tool in this activity) but don't see it in your toolbar, just right-click inside your toolbar. A full menu of tools will appear on screen. Drag the missing tool to your toolbar, and touch "Done."

Know Your Enemy

1. Display *Know Your Enemy* on the SMART Board and draw students' attention to the title. Ask students to think about who the "enemy" is when they write a persuasive essay. Guide students to understand that it is the "other side," people who have the opposite opinion of the writer.

2. Discuss with students: *Why should a writer care about the opposition?* Point out that it is possible that the reader has already heard arguments in favor of the other side. Maybe he or she is already leaning that way. If a writer knows the other side's arguments, the writer can knock them down and show why his or her side makes more sense.

3. Click on the right arrow to explore the example with the class. Explain that the text highlighted in green represents the other side's main argument. The text highlighted in yellow represents the writer's immediate response to that argument. Guide students to notice that the writer did not spend a lot of time giving details about the other side. Instead, the writer pointed out the opposition's argument quickly, then immediately shot it down with a powerful response.

4. Click on the right arrow and have a student volunteer use the SMART highlighter (green and yellow) to mark the opposing argument and writer's response in the paragraph about the movie. In SMART Notebook software, you'll find highlighters with multicolored ink in the pen tool menu.

5. Repeat step 4 for the other two pages.

6. Ask students to think about their own persuasive essay topics. Ask: *Does anyone have a topic where the other side has a strong argument? What could you say to counter, or argue against, that argument?*

7. Save your class's work and make a copy for each student's writing folder.

 TECH TIP

Remember that all digital ink, including pen and highlighter marks, can be erased easily with your SMART eraser. Select the eraser tool, then choose the width that will work best. Keep in mind that lines, shapes, and marks made with the Creative Pen cannot be removed with the eraser. Instead, they must be deleted using the red X on your toolbar.

Use Your Own Words

1. Though it can be difficult for young students to understand the concept of plagiarism, it is vital to address this issue when students are just beginning to research and write. Good habits instilled now will stay with students throughout their academic lives. In this activity, students will learn to recognize "stolen" words and to put arguments and details in their own words. Display *Use Your Own Words* on the SMART Board and read the introduction together. Discuss why it is important not to steal another writer's words.

2. Read the directions and demonstrate how to move a smiley face around on the page. Then, click on the right arrow to read aloud the official Doctors' Association Web site. Ask: *Can we tell that a group of doctors wrote this text? How? (The language sounds very scientific and adult. There are many words we do not recognize.)*

3. Direct students' attention to the three examples of student work on the next page. Have a volunteer read the first example aloud. Discuss whether the student managed to put the ideas into his or her own words. Ask: *Do you see strings of words that have been taken from the Web site? Does it sound like a kid could have written this? (In this case, the student did successfully put the material into his or her own words.)* If the student example gets a thumbs-up, have your student volunteer leave it alone. If it appears to have been plagiarized, have the volunteer drag the smiley face to the "jail" at the bottom of the page.

4. Repeat step 3 with the other two examples of student work. In example 2 (blue smiley face), guide students to notice the huge chunks of text that have been copied from the original Web site. Make sure your student volunteer places that writer in "jail"!

5. As students continue working on their own persuasive essays, remind them to make sure that they are putting all ideas into their own words.

EXTENDED LEARNING

Developing Arguments: Your Turn!

1. Print and make copies of *Developing Arguments: Your Turn!* Display the Notebook page on the SMART Board and distribute copies of the worksheet. Explain that students will complete this page on their own, either in class or for homework, to apply what they have learned about developing arguments for a persuasive essay. If students have already begun researching and writing their own essays, this page is an ideal tool for organizing and planning the body of the essay. If students have not yet begun their own projects, have them do the exercise for any persuasive topic on which they are well informed.

2. Review the directions, reminding students to:

> - Include three strong arguments.
>
> - Support those arguments with different kinds of details (definitions, facts, statistics, and examples).
>
> - Put all arguments and details in their own words.

   If students wish to address an opposing argument in the body of their essay, encourage them to describe the opposing view and offer a response on the back of the paper.

3. Once students have completed the activity, have partners share their work and provide feedback to one another.

Persuasive Techniques

By now, your students have learned the importance of having a strong stand and well-developed arguments. In this series of Notebook pages, they'll explore some tried-and-true persuasive techniques that can help them supplement their facts and win readers over!

OBJECTIVES

Students will be able to:

- ✓ Recognize persuasive techniques such as figurative language, loaded words, repetition, and bandwagon appeals.

- ✓ Know when to appropriately use persuasive techniques in their own writing.

TIME

About 3–4 class periods for Unit 4 (allow 15–20 minutes per lesson)

MEETING THE STANDARDS

This lesson correlates with the following writing standards for grades 3 through 6:

- Develop and demonstrate persuasive writing that is used for the purpose of influencing the reader.

- Include persuasive techniques (e.g., word choice, repetition).

GETTING READY

Before students arrive, have your SMART Board ready to go. Load the SMART Persuasive Writing CD onto your host computer and copy the **4 Persuasive Techniques** Notebook file onto your hard drive. Open the local file. The first interactive page, the *Persuasive Techniques* menu, will appear on your SMART Board. To display the Notebook pages for each of the eight lessons in this unit, click on the button next to the name of the lesson.

Tricks of the Trade

1. Display *Tricks of the Trade* on the SMART Board. Remind students that in ancient Greece, persuasion had three ingredients. *Ethos* involved having a trustworthy reputation, by knowing the facts and proving oneself. *Logos* involved using arguments and facts to build one's case. Explain that now, students will explore the third and final ingredient: *pathos*. Pathos is the recognition that feelings or emotions can help persuade a person. In persuasive writing, writers often use pathos by working in special tricks or techniques. Tell students they will probably recognize these tricks from commercials they see on TV!

2. Read the introduction aloud, and then click on the right arrow to go to the next page. Drag the Pull arrow to read the directions. Have a student volunteer read the persuasive writing challenge in the box at the top of the page.

3. Ask student volunteers to read aloud the five possible persuasive techniques. Discuss each one, focusing on why that particular appeal might sway some readers. For example:

    > • Point out that some people really idolize their favorite movie stars and singers, so technique 1 might work on them.
    >
    > • No one likes to feel excluded or different, so technique 2 might work on some.
    >
    > • Repeating a request over and over, as in technique 3, can be really annoying—or really effective!
    >
    > • In technique 4, words like *hero* and *selflessly* might make a reader feel honored or special.
    >
    > • Painting a picture of the problem in a person's mind is a great way to win them over. Discuss how the writer "paints pictures" in technique 5.

4. Follow up your discussion with a class vote. Tally which persuasive technique students think would work best on them. Use the SMART highlighter to highlight the winning technique.

5. Explain to students that each of these techniques has been used for thousands of years and that they will explore each one in further detail in the coming lessons. Before you move on, however, take a moment to emphasize that these techniques are meant to complement an already strong, logical essay. Discuss what an essay might look like if the writer used techniques like these instead of facts.

Say It Again! (Part 1)

1. Display *Say It Again! (Part 1)* on the SMART Board. Explain that this model essay uses one of the persuasive tricks students explored in the opening activity.

2. Read aloud the model essay clearly and slowly (including the title), encouraging students to listen for persuasive tricks.

3. If students notice any tricks, ask them to save their observations for Part 2 of this activity. Read the essay aloud a second time.

4. Follow this activity immediately with *Say It Again! (Part 2)*.

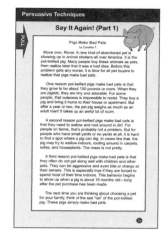

 **TECH TIP**

Looking for a place to record students' observations? In Notebook software, it's easy to find more room. Scroll down to the bottom of the activity page and click Extend Page. Use the extra white space to jot down your notes.

Say It Again! (Part 2)

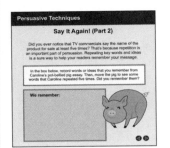

1. Display *Say It Again! (Part 2)* immediately after reading the model essay in Part 1. Explain that the model essay used the persuasive device of repetition, and that students will now evaluate the effectiveness of that technique.

2. Read the page introduction and directions. Guide students to understand that the key aspect of repetition is repeating the most important words and phrases—words and phrases the writer wants to stick in the reader's mind.

3. Have students reflect on Caroline's model essay from Part 1 and use SMART pens to jot down in the pink box any keywords or ideas that they recall.

4. Drag the pig away from its position on the page to reveal the expression that Caroline repeated five times in her essay: "Pigs make bad pets." Discuss whether students remembered this key idea. If not, return to Part 1 for a moment to search for this key phrase. Highlight it each time it appears.

5. Click on the right arrow and have students apply the concept of repetition to the essay ideas described on the page. For each thesis statement given, have students highlight some keywords or phrases that the writer could repeat for persuasive effect.

    Essay topic 1 (school schedule): Repeat "longer school day."

    Essay topic 2 (cell phones for soldiers): Repeat "American heroes" or "donate your old cell phone."

6. If students are working on their own persuasive essays, have them think about words or phrases they might repeat.

 TECH TIP

Use the Magic Pen to spotlight the words or phrases students think should be repeated. Choose the Magic Pen from your toolbar and use a finger to draw a circle around the desired word. The word will appear in a bright circle, while the rest of the page goes dark. Students find this captivating! To exit the spotlight, click on the red X.

Get on the Bandwagon!

1. Discuss the human tendency to want to be part of a group. Elicit examples of this in students' own lives—for example, times they felt they needed to get a new video game because "everyone else" had it or decided to join a dance class because all of their friends were joining. Point out that persuasive writers tap into that desire to belong by using something called *bandwagon appeals*.

2. Display *Get on the Bandwagon!* on the SMART Board and briefly discuss the origins of this unusual expression. Explain that back in the 1800s, circuses would travel around the country, performing in different towns and cities (much as they do today). Of course, there were no billboards or television ads back then. To get area residents interested in going to the circus, the circus master would arrange a colorful parade through town. The parade would include a horse-drawn wagon carrying a lively band playing music. People would follow the bandwagon to the circus rings. Now, the expression "jump on the bandwagon" is used to describe any time people go along with the crowd.

3. Read the introductory material and examples. Then click on the right arrow so students can read the four arguments on the next page. If an argument is a bandwagon appeal, have a volunteer drag the speaker onto the bandwagon.

4. Repeat with the remaining three arguments. In the end, you will have three characters on the bandwagon: the candidate running for election, the person talking about school uniforms, and the person advocating for the Earth Matters club. Discuss why the solar panel argument is NOT an example of a bandwagon appeal. *(It does not encourage the reader to be like everyone else.)*

5. Use the prompt at the bottom of the page to discuss whether students find bandwagon appeals particularly convincing.

Who Says?

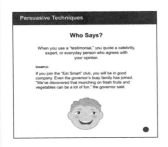

1. Introduce the testimonial technique by asking students to think of television ads they have seen starring celebrities. Ask: *Why would these companies use famous people to try to sell their products?* Explain that the companies want viewers to associate their products with someone whom they already like and trust.

2. Display *Who Says?* on the SMART Board and point out the three main sources of testimonials: celebrities, experts, and everyday people. In TV ads like those discussed above, celebrity testimonials are most common. But for a student writing a persuasive essay, it can be tough to find a star who supports the cause! In essays and letters, it is more common to include a testimonial from someone who knows a great deal about the topic (such as a doctor, scientist, or other expert) or someone who is affected by the problem or solution (an everyday person).

3. Click on the right arrow, then drag the Pull arrow to read the directions. Note that students will use the Creative Pen to put a star next to the most appropriate testimonial in each example.

4. Have students read the writing challenge and use the Creative Pen to star the best testimonial choice. (*The doctor who says that 9:00 p.m. is a reasonable bedtime*) Discuss why each of the other choices would not work well. (*A first grader's argument would not apply to a third grader; a singer and a senator probably don't know much about kids' sleep needs.*)

5. Click on the right arrow and repeat step 4 with the second writing challenge. Here, the best testimonial is probably from an everyday citizen who has witnessed accidents at the intersection. Again, talk about why the other choices do not make as much sense.

6. Save your class's work and make a copy of the pages for each student's writing folder.

 TECH TIP

Did more than one star shape appear when a student tapped the screen? The single tap can take some practice! To undo, simply click the undo tool as many times as is necessary.

Loaded Words

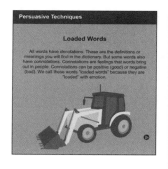

1. Display *Loaded Words* on the SMART Board and read aloud the introduction that explains connotations. Give an example or two to demonstrate how words can convey feelings. Say: *Imagine that it is 88 degrees outside and I say, "What a sunny day!" How is that different from saying, "What a scorching day!"? Would you feel better about* revising *a book report or* redoing *a book report?*

2. Click on the right arrow to go to the next page. Point out that the Word Box is organized into color-coded pairs. Each pair has one word with a positive connotation and one with a negative connotation. Read aloud the first pair (*disaster/challenge*) and demonstrate how to drag each word into the column where it belongs. Invite students to use each word in a sentence to get a feel for how loaded words change the meaning of a message. For example:

   • We could see that the fundraiser would be a *disaster*.

   • We could see that the fundraiser would be a *challenge*.

3. Have student volunteers continue with the remaining word pairs in the Word Box, putting each word in the appropriate column and using each one in a sentence.

4. Click on the right arrow to go to the Tips box. Read the tips aloud and help students see how they can apply loaded words to their own persuasive writing. Guide students to understand that overuse of loaded words distracts readers from an essay's strong, fact-based message.

5. Have students brainstorm other examples of loaded words (they need not be in pairs for this part of the exercise). You'll find some examples in the box below. Your students will undoubtedly come up with many others.

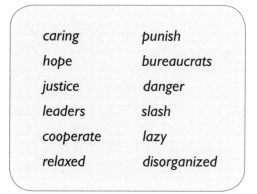

caring	punish
hope	bureaucrats
justice	danger
leaders	slash
cooperate	lazy
relaxed	disorganized

6. Save your class's work and make a copy for each student's writing folder.

TECH TIP

Remind students that when they are using the SMART Board and the selector tool is activated, their finger acts as a computer mouse! This allows them to drag text across the page.

Similes and Metaphors

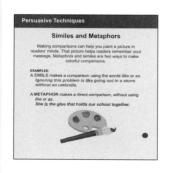

1. Review what your students already know about similes and metaphors and challenge them to name an example of each. Remind them that a simile makes a comparison using *like* or *as*. A metaphor makes a direct comparison without using *like* or *as*.

2. Display *Similes and Metaphors* on the SMART Board and read the introduction and examples together. Discuss why using similes and metaphors can help win readers over. (*It paints a picture in readers' heads that stays with them and helps them remember the writer's message.*)

3. Click on the right arrow and read the page directions. Have students read the first sentence and invite a volunteer to write *S* for simile, *M* for metaphor, or *N* for neither in the circle after the sentence. If the comparison is a simile, have the student circle the word *like* or *as*. (*Sentence 1 is a simile.*)

4. Repeat step 3 for the remaining seven sentences. (*Sentences 3, 4, and 6 are metaphors. Sentences 5 and 7 are similes. Sentences 2 and 8 are neither.*)

5. Have students begin brainstorming similes and metaphors they can use in their own persuasive essays.

6. Save your class's work and make a copy for each student's writing folder.

EXTENDED LEARNING

Persuasive Techniques: Your Turn!

1. Print and make copies of *Persuasive Techniques: Your Turn!* Display the Notebook page on the SMART Board and distribute copies of the worksheet. Explain that students will complete this page on their own, either in class or for homework, to apply what they have learned about persuasive techniques.

2. Review the directions with students, explaining that they will record their topic and thesis statement, then apply all five "tricks" to their own writing. Let students know that they should continue on the other side of the page if they run out of room. Students will:

> - Choose a word or phrase that could be repeated for persuasive effect.
> - Decide if a bandwagon appeal would work for their topic.
> - Decide what kind of testimonial they could use in their essay.
> - Name one or two words related to their topic and loaded with feeling.
> - Write a simile or metaphor that brings their topic to life in readers' minds.

3. Have students store their techniques in their writing notebook or folder and consult them when it is time to draft their persuasive essays.

The Traits of Good Writing

Your writers are in the home stretch! These Notebook pages will help them revise their persuasive essays for ideas, word choice, sentence fluency, organization, voice, and conventions.

OBJECTIVES

Students will be able to:

- ✓ Define the writing traits of ideas, word choice, sentence fluency, organization, voice, and conventions.
- ✓ Apply the traits of good writing to their own essays.

TIME

About 3–4 class periods for Unit 5 (allow 15–20 minutes per lesson)

MEETING THE STANDARDS

This lesson correlates with the following writing standards for grades 3 through 6:

- Apply a variety of composing and revision techniques used in the writing process.

- Establish central ideas, organization, elaboration, and unity in relation to purpose and audience.

- Revise writing to improve supporting details and word choice by adding or substituting text.

- Follow the rules of grammar, usage, spelling, and punctuation in persuasive writing.

- Proofread and edit writing for standard language conventions using checklists and other resources.

GETTING READY

Before students arrive, have your SMART Board ready to go. Load the SMART Persuasive Writing CD onto your host computer and copy the **5 The Traits of Good Writing** Notebook file onto your hard drive. Open the local file. The first interactive page, the *The Traits of Good Writing* menu, will appear on your SMART Board. To display the Notebook pages for each of the eight lessons in this unit, click on the button next to the name of the lesson.

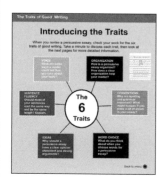

Introducing the Traits

1. Display *Introducing the Traits* on the SMART Board and wait a moment until the trait web stops spinning. Review what your students already know about the six traits of good writing.

2. Read and discuss the Organization prompt: *How is a persuasive essay organized? How does a clear organization help your reader?* Point out that students have already learned a lot about essay organization. They have learned that a lead and a thesis statement should appear in the first paragraph, followed by paragraphs centered on the main arguments, and then, finally, a closing paragraph that reiterates the thesis statement and matches the beginning. Point out that for readers, this sense of structure makes it easy to follow the essay. It is like driving with a map!

3. Read and discuss the Voice prompt: *What are some ways that a reader could tell that you care about your topic? (Possible answers include: I stated my opinion in a powerful way, my essay is full of feelings.)*

4. Read and discuss the Sentence Fluency prompt: *Should most of your sentences start the same way and be the same length? Explain.* Elicit from students that sentence variety keeps a piece of writing lively and interesting.

5. Read and discuss the Ideas prompt: *Why should a persuasive essay have a clear opinion statement and strong arguments?* Discuss how these main ideas form the backbone or substance of the essay. Without good ideas, the reader will feel shortchanged.

6. Read and discuss the Word Choice prompt: *What do you think about when you choose words for a persuasive essay?* Answers will vary widely, but guide students to think about words that are specific and "just right." Students may also recall the concept of emotionally "loaded" words from Unit 4.

7. Read and discuss the Conventions prompt: *Why are spelling and grammar important? What might happen if you made a lot of errors in your essay?* Point out that obvious mistakes make it appear as if the writer did not take care to polish the essay. The reader may wonder how much attention the writer paid to other aspects of the essay, such as researching ideas.

8. Explain to students that in this unit, they will explore some specific ways to revise their essays for these six traits.

TECH TIP

If animation tricks like the spinning idea web wow your students, add such tricks into any lesson you'd like! For example, as students write answers on the activity pages in this unit, make them spin or fade in and out. To animate a word, picture, or object, select the object, then go to the Properties menu and select Animation. Choose from the options provided to determine how the selected object will move, when it will move, and how quickly.

Clear Ideas

1. Display *Clear Ideas* on the SMART Board and read the directions together. Review that students will compare the two model essays to determine which one has strong, clear ideas. Remind students to ask: *Is it clear what the writer is trying to say? Is there a main idea here?*

2. Click on the right arrow to read aloud (or have a volunteer read aloud) the essay about cell-phone use at school. Ask: *What does the writer want us to think or do? Is it easy to find that message? What are the writer's main arguments?*

3. Repeat step 2 with the second essay about the stuffed animal collection. Discuss with students which essay has clearer ideas. Guide students to notice that this essay has a clear thesis: *"We are asking kids to donate their gently used plush animals for children in need."* It also has three clearly stated reasons: (1) You will be helping needy kids; (2) You will be helping local Girl Scouts; and (3) You will be cleaning out your playroom.

4. Have a student volunteer use the Creative Pen to put a star next to the second essay. Simply touch the Creative Pen tool with a finger, select the star pattern, and tap on the board to place the star.

5. Talk about ways the first writer could revise his or her essay about cell phones to make the ideas stand out more clearly. Sample responses: He or she could write a clear thesis statement instead of making general statements like, "it's not fair" and "they need to make the rules more fair." The writer should also make sure that each paragraph starts with a main idea.

💡 **TECH TIP**

Turn your stars into superstars! After placing a star on the screen, touch the selector tool (the plain black arrow) and then touch the star again. Touch the white resizing circle on the bottom right of the box and pull down and to the right.

Word Choice

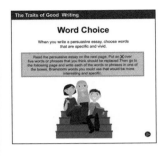

1. Ask students: *If I tell you, "It's time to do another thing,"* would you have any idea what I am talking about? Which writing trait do I need to work on? Point out that smart word choices can make writing shine. Then, change your instruction to, *"It's time to tackle another cool writing trait!"*

2. Display *Word Choice* on the SMART Board and read the directions together. Clarify that students may spot more than five words that should be replaced, but that, for now, they will find and focus on five of the worst offenders.

3. Model how to put an *X* mark on the screen. Go to the Shapes icon and select the *X* with your finger. Now, each time you tap the screen, an *X* will appear.

4. Click on the right arrow to go to the next page. Have students read the model essay about litter and identify words or phrases that are lifeless, generic, and dull. Have them touch each word with a finger to place an *X* on top of it.

5. Click on the right arrow to go to the next page and then click on the Single/ Dual Page Display icon to display both pages at once. Have students select five words to work with and write them in the boxes on the right screen. Together, brainstorm possible replacements that are more specific and lively. Some ideas are listed below.

> **Consider replacing these words and phrases:**
>
> **area** (grounds, property)
>
> **pieces of trash** (cans, plastic bags, wrappers, etc.)
>
> **stuff like that** (see above)
>
> **this thing** (problem, issue, embarrassment)
>
> **be over** (change to active voice: time for students to address—or solve, fix, tackle—this problem)
>
> **not very good** (damaging, dangerous, devastating)
>
> **look bad** (look uncaring, irresponsible, disrespectful to the planet)
>
> **really good about** (proud of)

 TECH TIP

Did you somehow end up with *X*'s all over the page while demonstrating this function to your class? Lose unwanted *X*'s (or other shapes) by clicking back on the plain black arrow. Touch the shape you want to delete and then touch the red *X* (Delete tool) in your Notebook toolbar. You can also hit the back arrow as many times as is necessary to clear the unwanted shapes.

Sentence Fluency

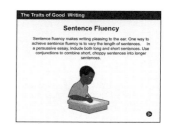

1. Display *Sentence Fluency* on the SMART Board and review with students that sentence fluency is the trait that makes writing pleasing to the ear. The sentences seem to flow together. Explain that one way to achieve sentence fluency is to vary the length of sentences. If all of a writer's sentences are short, the essay can sound choppy and awkward. Too many long sentences can sound boring.

2. Click on the right arrow and read the directions and Kevin's essay aloud. Ask students if they think this essay is pleasing to the ear. Click on the right arrow to go to the next page. Explain that the colorful words featured here are called *conjunctions*. They can be used to combine sentences. Demonstrate how to move one of the conjunctions by dragging it across the page with a finger.

3. Have a student volunteer read the first pair of short sentences and use a replace-and-check technique to see which of the conjunctions makes the most sense in context. Invite the student to drag the appropriate word to the white box between the two short sentences.

4. Repeat step 3 with the remaining pairs of sentences on the following pages. Your students will create five new, longer sentences, as follows:

   - Kids today are busy, BUT surely they can find a little time to help out.
   - Raking leaves is easy, AND it is a great way to help an elderly neighbor. (Accept SO or BUT here as well.)
   - Some senior citizens need help with yardwork BECAUSE they have arthritis or other health problems.
   - I know kids care about their neighbors, SO they should make an effort to help as much as possible.
   - Kids might even feel better about themselves WHEN they help others in their community.

5. Use the question on the last page to prompt students to think of other ways to increase sentence variety. Examples include starting with different words and phrases and mixing together different kinds of sentences (questions, exclamations, and statements).

All About Organization

1. In this activity, students will explore two key aspects of organization: avoiding extraneous details that might sidetrack the reader and making sure the essay ending circles back to the beginning. Display *All About Organization* on the SMART Board and read the introduction and page directions. Then click on the right arrow and have students take turns reading the paragraphs in Lucia's model essay.

2. Challenge students to raise their hands when they hear a detail that just doesn't seem to belong. Pause after each paragraph to invite students to point out these details. (*Note: Paragraph 1 does not include any irrelevant details.*) As students point out extraneous, irrelevant details, use the SMART pen to cross each detail out. Students should identify the following unnecessary details:

> • Just hope that the person in front of you is not so tall that they block your view, like the one in front of me was when I went.
>
> • I think it must be hard to be an actor or actress.
>
> • I just got a computer program that lets you do little special effects, and it is kind of fun to use.

3. Discuss why unrelated details are a bad idea. (*They throw readers off track and distract from the main message.*)

4. Draw students' attention to the beginning and ending of the essay. Have them describe ways that the writer connects these two important parts. (*The writer repeats her thesis statement urging readers to see the movie as soon as possible and circles back to the idea of not bothering to buy popcorn.*)

5. Invite students who already have written their essay beginnings to share them with the class. Collaborate to come up with ways each writer could circle back to his or her lead at the end of the essay.

Find Your Voice

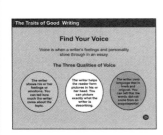

1. Explain that voice is one of the hardest traits to define because it includes little bits of the other traits. In general, writing with a strong voice helps readers recognize the writer's personality. The writer reveals a bit of himself or herself by sharing strong feelings, offering vivid examples and images, and choosing words that someone else might not choose.

2. Display *Find Your Voice* on the SMART Board and read the introduction. Walk students through the three qualities of voice listed in the circles on the page. (Quality 3 mentions "words that don't sound like they came from an encyclopedia." If your students are unfamiliar with voiceless encyclopedia writing, pull out a volume or log on to read a paragraph out loud!)

3.	Click on the right arrow to go to the next page. Drag the Pull arrow to review the directions and then read aloud the model persuasive letter about Amazing Math Day. You may want to read the letter twice so that students can absorb the language.

4.	Have students match each quality of voice to one or more spots in the story where that quality is evident. Students can use the SMART highlighter to highlight these spots in a color that matches the appropriate circle.

> **Writer shows emotions; you can tell that he or she cares about the topic:**
>
> > *enthusiastically*
> >
> > *I humbly ask*
> >
> > *thrilling, real-life setting*
> >
> > *I can proudly say*
> >
> > *this deserving class*

> **Writer helps reader form mental pictures:**
>
> > *their faces lit up like Christmas trees*
> >
> > *scream-inspiring drops*
> >
> > *soar with the birds*

> **Writer uses language that is fresh and original:**
>
> > *zip, zoom, and spin around*
> >
> > *one-of-a-kind opportunity*
> >
> > *puzzle out the perimeter . . . as they puff and chug along*
> >
> > *make the clear choice*

 TECH TIP

If you're using the SMART Board with younger students, move the toolbar to the bottom of the screen so they can more conveniently reach shapes, lines, and other tools. Just click on the vertical up-and-down arrow that appears at the end of the toolbar.

5.	Go around the room and have students share one emotion that they hope will be evident in their essays OR one particularly lively or interesting word or expression that they will use.

6.	Save your class's work and make a copy for each student's writing folder.

Conventions Count

1. Ask students if they have ever noticed mistakes on menus, signs, and other public places, and what they thought of the business after they noticed. Point out that mistakes in spelling, capitalization, or punctuation can make business patrons question the quality of a business—and can make essay readers wonder if there are mistakes or careless errors elsewhere in the text. Mistakes undermine the persuasive message by showing the reader that the writer did not care enough about the topic to polish his or her writing.

2. Display *Conventions Count* on the SMART Board. Point out the three types of errors students will be looking for: spelling, capitalization, and punctuation. Click on the right arrow and direct students' attention to the Proofreading Marks box on the page. Explain that students will read an essay and then use the red SMART pen to make these marks when they find errors.

3. Click on the right arrow to go to the next page and then click on the Single/ Dual Page Display icon to display both pages at once. Read the essay one paragraph at a time. Pause after each paragraph so that student volunteers can approach the SMART Board and correct errors using the proofreading marks. We found 16 mistakes, so there are plenty of opportunities for participation!

4. Save your class's work and make a copy for each student's writing folder. Encourage students to use the same marks to proofread their own essays.

EXTENDED LEARNING

The Traits of Good Writing: Your Turn!

1. Print and make copies of *The Traits of Good Writing: Your Turn!* Display the Notebook page on the SMART Board and distribute copies of the worksheet. Explain that students will use this checklist of writing traits to revise their own persuasive essays, either in class or for homework. Now is an ideal time for students to create polished versions of their essays using a word processor.

2. Have students attach the completed checklist to their finished essays. Use the checklist yourself to evaluate and discuss students' persuasive essays.